# 'TWAS THE NIGHT BEFORE CHRISTMAS

## Early Santa History Plus Rare 1821 Children's Friend With Old Santeclaus

## 'TWAS THE NIGHT SERIES BOOK 1

**JULEANNE CRIGHTON**

Copyright © 2019 by Juleanne Crighton

All rights reserved. No part may be reproduced, copied, transmitted, or stored in any form without written permission of the publisher.

Published by RW Classics, 2019. publisher@rwclassics.com

Cover design by Robert G. Miller. Santa images on cover and table of contents illustrated by Thomas Nast, from *The Night Before Christmas, or, A Visit of St. Nicholas*. New York: McLoughlin Brothers, *circa* 1896, 6-7.

*'Twas the Night Before Christmas: Early Santa History Plus Rare 1821 Children's Friend With Old Santeclaus* ('Twas the Night Series Book 1) includes a history of Santa and his reindeer, notes, bibliography, illustrations and *The Children's Friend: A New-Year's Present, to the Little Ones From Five to Twelve* with *Old Santeclaus Poem. Part III* illustrated by Arthur J. Stansbury, originally published by William B. Gilley in 1821. All illustrations meticulously updated to remove pixelations, dust, and debris.

Names: Crighton, Juleanne, author.

Title: 'Twas the night before christmas: early santa history plus 1821 rare children's friend with old santeclaus ('twas the night series book 1) / Juleanne Crighton.

Description: Murrieta, CA : RW Classics, 2019 : illustrations updated with pixelations, dust, and debris removed.

Identifiers: ISBN 978-1-946100-25-2 (hardcover) | ISBN 978-1-946100-26-9 (pbk) | ISBN 978-1-946100-28-3 (large print pbk) | ISBN 978-1-946100-27-6 (ebook)

# CONTENTS

**PART I: EARLY HISTORY OF SANTA AND HIS REINDEER** .................. 9
   Early History of Santa Claus and Reindeer Introduction ........... 11
   Saint Nicholas to America ............................................. 13
   First Mention of Santa Claus ......................................... 14
   Santaclaus, Presents, Stockings (Washington Irving) ................ 14
   Santa in Art Form (John Pintard) .................................... 16
   Sancte Claus Poem .................................................... 18
   Santa in Flying Wagon (Washington Irving) ........................... 19
   Earliest Visual of Santa in Sleigh with One Flying Reindeer ........ 19
   NEW Santa and Eight Reindeer ........................................ 20
   First Time Santa and Eight Reindeer in Newsprint ................... 21
   Expanded Version of Santa (James K. Paulding) ....................... 22
   Dunder and Blixem Reindeer Names Changed ............................ 23
   First Time Santa and Reindeer Featured in Harper's ................. 25

**PART II: RARE 1821 CHILDREN'S FRIEND WITH OLD SANTECLAUS** .......... 33
   Introduction to Part II .............................................. 35
   Old Santeclaus with Much Delight .................................... 37
   The Steady Friend of Virtuous Youth ................................. 38
   Through Many Houses He Has Been ..................................... 39
   Where E'er I Found Good Girls or Boys ............................... 40
   To Some I Gave a Pretty Doll ........................................ 41
   No Drums to Stun Their Mother's Ear ................................. 42
   But Where I Found the Children Naughty .............................. 43
   I Left a Long, Black, Birchen Rod ................................... 44

**'TWAS THE NIGHT SERIES** ............................................. 46
**BIBLIOGRAPHY** ....................................................... 48

# LIST OF ILLUSTRATIONS

| | |
|---|---|
| Santa and Reindeer Flying Over Treetops, circa 1872 by Thomas Nast... | 7 |
| A Visit From St. Nicholas, 1879 by Frederick B. Schell | 10 |
| Washington Irving, 1848 by James D. Smillie from F. O. C. Darley | 15 |
| St. Nicholas Broadside Engraving, 1810 by Alexander Anderson | 17 |
| Santa and Reindeer, circa 1830 by Bryon King | 21 |
| Clement Clarke Moore's Handwritten Changes to Poem, 1844 | 24 |
| A Visit from Saint Nicholas, 1857 by Felix Octavius Carr Darley | 26 |
| Various Santa Poses, 1857 (artist unknown, three illustrations) | 27 |
| Thomas Nast's First Published Santa Illustrations (two) | 29 |
| Santa Claus, Merry Christmas, 1885 by Thomas Nast | 30 |
| Merry Old Santa Claus, 1881 by Thomas Nast | 31 |
| Cover of The Children's Friend, 1821 | 36 |
| Santa and One Reindeer, 1821 by Arthur J. Stansbury | 37 |
| Santeclaus, 1821 by Arthur J. Stansbury | 38 |
| Santa and Stockings, 1821 by Arthur J. Stansbury | 39 |
| Excited Children, 1821 by Arthur J. Stansbury | 40 |
| Mischievous Children, 1821 by Arthur J. Stansbury | 41 |
| Family, Reading Book, 1821 by Arthur J. Stansbury | 42 |
| Children Being Naughty, 1821 by Arthur J. Stansbury | 43 |
| Stockings With Switches, 1821 by Arthur J. Stansbury | 44 |
| Back Cover of The Children's Friend, 1821 | 45 |

A vivid illustration of Santa Claus flying over treetops and houses with his reindeer by Thomas Nast. The illustration was featured in *Aunt Lousa's big picture series, A Visit of St. Nicholas*, published circa 1872, eleven years after Clement Clarke Moore's death.

# PART I

## Part I: Early History of Santa and His Reindeer

A VISIT FROM ST. NICHOLAS.

Santa Claus illustrated by Frederick B. Schell. Source: Henry T. Coates, ed., *The Children's Book of Poetry: Carefully Selected From the Works of the Best and Most Popular Writers for Children*, (Philadelphia: Porter & Coates, 1879), 394.

## Early History of Santa Claus and His Reindeer

Our beloved Santa Claus made his way into American culture by way of an archbishop named Saint Nicholas. Born around 280 A.D., by all accounts St. Nicholas was a native of Patara, in Lycia (which is now Turkey). Pure, devoted, and obedient even as infant, Nicholas observed Church-appointed fast days by refusing his mothers' milk on Wednesday's and Friday's. His parents died when he was young and left him great riches and he pledged his inheritance to works of charity. Over the years, St. Nicholas devoted himself to a religious life in the Holy Sion monastery, near Myra, where he was appointed Abbot by the Archbishop. Later, one of the metropolitan churches became vacant and he was chosen as archbishop, which he served until his death. In that position, he became famous for extraordinary piety and zeal, and for a large number of miracles.

One miracle often attributed to St. Nicholas, although more charity than miracle, is when he saved three young daughters of a poor noblemen from ill repute, where the father planned to send them in exchange for bread. The father had no money for dowries for his daughter due to his poverty and therefore he was unable to find each a husband. St. Nicholas became aware of the dire situation and under the cover of darkness, he threw a bag filled with gold through the window of the poor man's house that could be used for a dowry. Soon, the eldest daughter married and St. Nicholas threw in another bag of gold then the middle daughter married. For the youngest daughter, the father stood watch and when St. Nicholas threw in the last bag of gold the poor man overwhelmed him with gratitude.[1]

In another, legend has it that St. Nicholas commanded the sea and it obeyed him. As the story goes, St. Nicholas sailed for the Holy Land to visit holy places in Jerusalem. The sky was clear and the sea calm but St. Nicholas told the sailors to

---

[1] S. Baring-Gould, *The Lives of the Saints*, (London: John Hodges, 1877), 65.

prepare for a great storm. When the storm came, the sailors begged him to save the ship from wreck. St. Nicholas prayed. The winds subsided and the sea calmed. On the voyage home, the mariners wanted to sail into Alexandria and when St. Nicholas discovered that, he prayed. The wind shifted, and the ship sailed to Lycia instead.[2]

After elected bishop of Myra, a woman brought into the church her child who had fallen into a fire. St. Nicholas made a sign of a cross over the burned child and restored him to health.

St. Nicholas suffered imprisonment for his faith. Persecuted by Roman emperor Diocletian, Saint Nicholas made a glorious confession at a time when Christians were persecuted and was imprisoned but later set free by Emperor Constantine.

History places his death in 342 A.D.,[3] Myra, where he was buried in his cathedral.[4] "No saint was more universally honoured in all Christian nations than St. Nicholas." He was one of the most faithful that ever served the Church. Upon his death, relics of the saint were kept in Myra then later moved to the church of St. Stephen in Italy, May 1087. Eyewitnesses state that on the first day his remains arrived, thirty people were cured of various distempers.[5]

Saint Nicholas was deemed a patron of children because he made their instruction a principle part of his pastoral care. He retained children's good virtues throughout his adulthood. He was meek, simple, and without guile or malice, all qualities of innocent children.[6]

---

[2] Ebenezer Cobham Brewer, *A Dictionary of Miracles: Imitative, Realistic, and Dogmatic with Illustrations,* (Philadelphia, PA: J. B. Lippincott Company, 1894), 286.
[3] Alban Butler, Rev., *The Lives of the Fathers Martyrs, and Other Principal Saints; Compiled from Original Monuments, and other Authentic Records, Illustrated with The Remarks of Judiciuos Modern Critics and Historians, Vol. II,* (London: Joseph Booker, 1833), 988-89.
[4] Alban Butler, Rev., *The Lives of,* 988-89.
[5] Alban Butler, Rev., *The Lives of,* 989.
[6] Alban Butler, Rev., *The Lives of,* 990.

According to legend, St. Nicholas left gifts for good children and switches for those who were bad. The day of his death on December 6, became an annual celebration called, St. Nicholas Day. By the Renaissance period, Nicholas was the "most popular saint in Europe,"[7] referred to as Father Christmas in England.

## 1600's

### Saint Nicholas to America

When Dutch colonists migrated to America in the 1600s they brought along with them the legend of their beloved Saint Nicholas, whom they affectionately called Sinter Klaas or Santer Klause. They set sail from Amsterdam for the shores of America in the *Goede Vrouw* (good woman) with one hundred feet each in the keel, in the beam, and from the bottom of the sternpost to the tafforel. The vessel, declared the greatest belle in Amsterdam, had an enormous pair of cat-heads, copper, and withal—'a most prodigious poop!' said American author, Washington Irving, writing as Diedrich Knickerbocker. On the head was a "goodly image of St. Nicholas, with a low, broad-brimmed hat, a huge pair of Flemish trunk hose,[8] and a pipe that reached to the end of the bow-spirit." Rightfully so, the gallantly furnished ship floated sideways "like a majestic goose."[9]

The Dutch colony of New Netherland was established in 1624, which is now New York City and parts of Long Island, New Jersey, and Connecticut. Southern Manhattan Island, New York, became New Amsterdam during the migration. New Amsterdam passed on to English rule in the mid 1600s and in 1665 was

---

[7] "Santa Claus," *History*, www.history.com/topics/christmas/santa-claus, (July 6, 2019).
[8] Wide, baggy breeches of Dutch origin.
[9] Washington Irving [writing as Diedrich Knickerbocker], *A History of New-York From the Beginning of the World to the End of the Dutch Dynasty, Vol. I*, (New York: Inskeep & Bradford, 1809), 78. *History* is a New York history book filled with light-hearted satire.

reincorporated as New York City. Through the years as migrants and their families adopted the english language, Sinter Klaas became Santa Claus.

## 1773

### First Mention of Santa Claus

In 1883, Rivington's *New-York Gazetteer* printed a notice with the first mention of Santa Claus (as St. a Claus) on December 23. The notice read: "Last Monday the anniversary of St. Nicholas, otherwise called St. a Claus, was celebrated at Protestant Hall, at Mr. Waldron's, where a great number of the Sons of that ancient Saint celebrated the day, with great joy and festivity."

## 1808-1809

### 'Santaclaus,' Presents, and Stockings (Washington Irving)

New York author Washington Irving is often credited for promoting St. Nicholas and family traditions. Best known for *Rip Van Winkle* (1819) and *The Legend of Sleepy Hollow* (1820), Irving penned several satirical and serious books. In one, he reflected on his grandfather's good old days, when he said cakes (cookies) had an image on one side of Rip Van Dam and the other side, St. Nicholas, 'vulgarly called Santaclaus.'[10]

His book, *A History of New York,* was a playful parody purposely published on St. Nicholas Day, December 6, 1809,[11] the same year he became a member of the

---

[10] Washington Irving [writing as Diedrich Knickerbocker], *Salmagundi: or, The Whim Whams and Opinions of Launcelot Langstaff, Esq. and Others* [No. XX-Monday, January 25, 1808 "From My Elbow Chair"], (London: T. Davison, Whitefriars, 1824), 368.

[11] Charles W. Jones, "Knickerbocker Santa Claus," *St. Nicholas Center,* May 16, 2019, www.stnicholascenter.org/who-is-st-nicholas/origin-of-santa/kickerbocker.

New York Historical Society. In it, he reminded readers of traditions on the day of St. Nicholas, which included making presents and stockings hung in the chimney.[12] He dedicated it to the New York Historical Society. Irving revised the *History of New York* three times (1812, 1819, and 1848) and founded the St. Nicholas Society in 1835.

**Etched by James D. Smillie after a sketch from the life by F. O. C. Darley at Sunnyside, July 1848. Source: Evert A. Duyckinck, *Irvingiana: A Memorial of Washington Irving*, (New York: C.B. Richardson, 1860), frontpiece.**

---

[12] Washington Irving [writing as Diedrich Knickerbocker], *A History of New-York From the Beginning of the World to the End of the Dutch Dynasty, Vol. II*, (New York: Inskeep & Bradford, 1809), 252.

## 1810

### Santa in Art Form (John Pintard)

The following year, Santa Claus appeared in art form when fellow New York Historical Society member, John Pintard, promoted Saint Nicholas as a patron saint by commissioning artist Alexander Anderson to create woodcut broadsides of the saint for the first anniversary celebration of the Festival of Saint Nicholas, held December 6, 1810. The woodcut broadside featured a stern Saint Nicholas on the left—barefoot, robed, and holding a switch—and to the right was a 'good' little girl who stood on the fireplace mantel directly over a stocking filled with toys and a 'bad' little boy who stood to her right, wiping tears from his face—his stocking filled with switches. A "St. Nicholas, good, holy man!" poem appeared at the bottom, both in Dutch and English. It read:

> SAINT NICHOLAS, good holy man!
> Put on the Tabard [kind of jacket], best you can,
> Go, clad therewith, to Amsterdam,
> From Amsterdam to Hispanje,
> Where apple bright [orange] of Oranje,
> And likewise those granate [Pomegranates] surnam'd,
> Roll through the streets, all free unclaim'd.
> SAINT NICHOLAS, my dear good friend!
> To serve you ever was my end,
> If you will, now, me something give,
> I'll serve you ever while I live.

Part I: Early History of Santa and His Reindeer

1810 broadside engraving by Alexander Anderson distributed for the New York Historical Society at its first celebration of the Festival of St. Nicholas, December 6, 1810 [courtesy of New York Historical Society Library].

Less than two weeks later, on December 12, 1810, the *New York Commercial Advertiser* published the first American poem that named St. Nicolas 'Sancte Claus.' Parts of the anonymous poem are similar to both Washington Irving's *History of New York* and John Pintard's 1810 St. Nicholas broadside.

### A Paraphrase of the Dutch Hymn to Saint Nicholas

Oh good holy man! whom we *Sancte Claus* name,
The Nursery forever your praise shall proclaim:
The day of your joyful revisit returns,
When each little bosom with gratitude burns,
For the gifts which at night you so kindly impart,
To the girls of your love, and the boys of your heart.
Oh! come with your panniers and pockets well stow'd,
Our stockings shall help you to lighten your load,
As close to the fire-side gaily they swing,
While delighted we dream of the presents you bring.

Oh! bring the bright Orange so juicy and sweet,
Bring Almonds and Raisins to heighten the treat;
Rich *Waffles* and *Dough-Nuts* must not be forgot,
Nor *Crullers* and *Oley-Cooks* fresh from the pot.
But of all these fine presents your Saintship can find,
Oh! leave not the famous big *Cookies* behind.
Or if in your hurry one thing you mislay,
Let that be the *Rod*—and ah! keep it away.

Then holy Saint Nicholas! all the long year,
Our books we will love and our parents revere;
From naughty behaviour we'll always refrain,
In hopes that you'll come and reward us again.

## 1812

### Santa in Flying Wagon (Washington Irving)

In Washington Irving's 1812 revision of *A History of New York*, he referred to Saint Nicholas as soaring over treetops in a flying wagon. His 1819 edition read, "And the sage Oloffe dreamed a dream—and lo, the good St. Nicholas came riding over the tops of the trees, in that self same wagon wherein he brings his yearly presents to children."[13]

## 1821

### Earliest Visual of Santa in Sleigh with One Flying Reindeer
### [INCLUDED in Part II: The Children's Friend]

William B. Gilley published *The Children's Friend, Number III, A New-Year's Present to the Little Ones from Five to Twelve* in 1821. The book included an Old Santeclaus poem coupled with eight color illustrations. Although the author of *Children's Friend* remained anonymous, some speculate the author could be James K. Pauling, who wrote a full-length book in 1834 about Santa, or Arthur J. Stansburg, the illustrator. But others believe the infamous Clement Clarke Moore, who authored the world's famous 'Twas the Night Before Christmas poem, was the author. It's important to note; however, Professor Moore never claimed the Old Santeclaus poem. Regardless of its author, there is no doubt the 1821 poem influenced Moore in writing 'Twas the Night Before Christmas as it was the first time a flying reindeer appeared on paper.

---

[13] Washington Irving, *A History of New-York, Vol. I*, 135.

## 1823

## NEW Santa and Eight Flying Reindeer

The most endearing Christmas poem of all time was first published anonymously in the New York *Troy Sentinel*, December 23, 1823. *A Visit From St. Nicholas*, known for the first line in the verse, "'Twas the night before Christmas," invented a wonderful new image of Santa Claus that children could relate to. He went from a slender bishop to the jolly, plump, likable Santa we know today. "He had a broad face, and a little round belly, that shook, when he laughed, like a bowl full of jelly."

The poem was a runaway hit and media published the classic annually at Christmas, but people were curious. Who wrote it? In 1829, the *Troy Sentinal* republished the poem with hints of the author's identity:

"The lines were *first* published in this paper. By birth and residence, to the City of New York, and that he is a gentleman of *more* merit as a scholar and a writer than many of more noisy pretensions."[14] The description fit poet Clement Clarke Moore, a professor at New York's General Theological Seminary, to a tee. According to scholar Scott Norsworthy, when the *Troy Sentinal* reprinted the piece in 1829, editor Orville L. Holley already knew who wrote it, which Holley verified in a news article.[15] Moore soon confirmed authorship and included the poem in a collection of his own.

The new Santa now had eight flying reindeer instead of one. Moore named them: Dasher, Dancer, Prancer, Vixen, Comet, Cupid, Dunder, and Blixem, the last two names, of which, would soon change.

---

[14] Seth Kaller, "Appendix C: Historical Timeline," *Seth Kaller, Inc.,* May 12, 2019, www.sethkaller.com/about/educational/tnbc-2.

[15] Scott Norsworthy, "First printing of A Visit from St. Nicholas," *Melvilliana,* April 8, 2019, https://melvilliana.blogspot.com/2019/04/first-printing-of-visit-from-st-nicholas.html.

Part I: Early History of Santa and His Reindeer

1830 (circa)

## First Time Santa and Eight Reindeer in Newsprint

Shown here, is a copy of a woodcut made by Troy New York engraver, Myron King, who created an engraving based on Moore's new Santa and eight reindeer. It is believed to be the <u>first</u> illustration of Santa with eight reindeer.

First known illustration of Santa with eight reindeer based on *A Visit From St. Nicholas* poem by artist Myron King, circa 1830. Source. Courtesy of Troy Public Library, New York.

## 1834

## Expanded Version of Santa (James K. Paulding)

Washington Irving's close friend, James Kirke Paulding (August 22, 1778 - April 6, 1860), who was a member of the Board of Navy Commissioners from 1815 to 1823 and later became secretary of the Navy 1838 to 1841, elaborated on Irving's description of St. Nicholas when he wrote a full-length book about the saint called, *The Story Book of Saint Nicholas* in 1834.[16] He wrote:

". . . I was favoured with the appearance of a vision, which, at first sight, I knew to be that of the excellent St. Nicholas . . . He is a right fat, jolly, roistering little fellow—if I may make bold to call him so familiarly . . . He was dressed in a snuff-coloured coat of goodly conceited dimension, having broad skirts, cuffs might to behold and buttons about the size of a moderate Newyear cooky . . . his shoes . . . ornamented with a pair of silver buckles, exceedingly bright." Paulding wrote in satire as Irving did and said the saint spoke to him in Dutch and commanded him to write the book (and even gave him the title) so he could have a stronghold in the New World. In the first part of his book, Paulding described the legend of St. Nicholas.

"St. Nicholas was born—and that is all I can tell of the matter—on the first of January; but in what year or at what place, are facts which I have not been able to ascertain . . . Nothing is known of his early youth, except that it hath come down to us that his mother dreamed the night before his birth, that the sun was changed into a vast Newyear cake . . . Little Nicholas, our hero, was a merry, sweet-tempered caitiff, which was, doubtless, somewhat owing to his living almost altogether upon sweet things. He was marvellously devoted to cakes, and ate up numberless gingerbread alphabets before he knew a single letter." Nicholas was a

---

[16] James K. Paulding, *The Story Book of Saint Nicholas Translated From the Original Dutch of Dominie Nicholas Aegidius Oudenarde.* (New York: Harper & Brothers, 1836), 13-32.

baker growing up. He married and lived happily many years together, "But it was ordained that he never should be blessed with any offspring, seeing that he predestined to be the patron and benefactor of the children of others."

"Everybody knows the excellent St. Nicholas, in holyday times, goes about among the people in the middle of the night, distributing all sorts of toothsome and becoming gifts to the good boys and girls . . . some say that he comes down the chimneys in a little Jersey wagon; others, that he wears a pair of Holland skates, with which he travels like the wind; and others, who pretend to have seen him, maintain that he has lately adopted a locomotive, and was once actually detected on the Albany railroad."

"St. Nicholas, thrice blessed soul! was riding up one chimney and down another like a locomotive engine in his little one-horse wagon, distributing cakes to the good boys, and whips to the bad ones."[17]

### 1844

### Dunder and Blixem Reindeer Names Changed

On February 26, 1844, Clement Clarke Moore wrote to the *Troy Sentinel* publisher prior to the newspaper re-printing his celebrated poem that year. Moore provided the publisher with corrections on the back of a broadside copy of the poem. Among his changes was to correct the name of one reindeer. Moore crossed out *Blixem* and wrote *Blitzen*,[18] which remains the official spelling today.

---

[17] Paulding. *The Story Book,* 149.
[18] Emily Chapin, "Clement Clarke Moore and Santa in the City," *Museum of the City of New York,* 222.mcny.org/story/clement-clarke-moore-and-santa-city (November 29, 2016).

> And he whistled, and shouted, and called them by name;
> "Now, *Dasher!* now, *Dancer!* now, *Prancer* and *Vixen!*
> On, *Comet!* on, *Cupid!* on, *Dunder* and ~~Blixem~~ *Blitzen!*
> To the top of the porch! to the top of the wall!
> Now dash away! dash away! dash away all!"
> As dry leaves that before the wild hurricane fly,

Clement Clarke Moore's handwritten change to the reindeer name in 1844.
Courtesy of Museum of the City of New York, call no. 54.331.17.

In March of the same year, Moore formally acknowledged authorship of the 1823 *A Visit from St. Nicholas* poem by including it within his own book of poems. Although he did not alter the reindeer spelling of *Dunder* in handwritten changes given to the *Troy Sentinel* publisher in February, *Dunder* became *Donder* in his book of poems.[19] No one is a hundred percent sure how or when *Donder* changed to *Donner*, the reindeer name we know today. But by 1850 a reference to Professor Moore's *Donner* appeared in *Rural Hours by a Lady*, a journal written by Susan Fenimore Cooper.[20]

"It is well for Santa Claus that we have snow. If we may believe Mr. Moore, who has seen him nearer than most people, he travels in a miniature sleigh, With eight tiny rein-deer: Now Dasher, now Dancer! Now Prancer, now Vixen! On Cupid, on Cornet [typographical error—should be Comet] On Donner and Blixen!"

---

[19] Clement C. Moore, LL. D. *Poems*, (New York: Bartlett & Welford, 1844), 125.
[20] Susan Fenimore Cooper, *Rural Hours by a Lady*, (New York: George P. Putnam, 1850), 436. Susan Cooper was the daughter of the well known novelist James Fenimore Cooper, author of *The Last of the Mohicans*.

A search of the Library of Congress revealed the earliest known date a newspaper published the change to *Donner* was December 26, 1891.[21]

1857

### First Time Santa and Reindeer Featured in *Harper's*

The first time Santa and his reindeer appeared in *Harper's* with wide distribution was in 1857. Prominently featured on the cover of *Harper's New Monthly Magazine*, the illustration showed Santa climbing into the chimney while his reindeer waited nearby. The illustration accompanied Moore's 'Twas the Night poem but was unsigned by its artist. A quick research of *The Poets of the Nineteenth Century*, where the poems for *Harper's* came from (as shown on its cover), revealed Moore's *Visit* poem and the Santa drawing, illustrated by F. O. C. Darley.[22] Felix Octavius Carr Darley was an American artist best known for illustrations in works by authors such as Charles Dickens, Clement Clarke Moore, Washington Irving, and Henry Wadsworth Longfellow, among others. Harper's separate publication, *Harper's Weekly*, featured uncredited illustrations of Santa in various poses in the December 26th edition of the same year. The illustrations are displayed on the following pages.

---

[21] "Holiday Greeting, Our Annual Supplement (supplement to the Thibodaux L.A. Sentinel)," *The Weekly Thibodaux Sentinel and Journal of the 8th Senatorial District*, December 26, 1891.

[22] Robert Aris Willmott, ed., *The Poets of the Nineteenth Century*, (New York: Harper & Brothers, 1858), xiv, 288-90. Note: though published in 1858, this book was entered, according to the act of Congress, in 1857, the same year Harper's magazine featured the poem and illustration.

# NEW MONTHLY MAGAZINE.

No. XCI.—DECEMBER, 1857.—Vol. XVI.

## A Christmas Garland of American Poems.

[From "The Poets of the Nineteenth Century." 8vo. Superbly Illustrated. Harper & Brothers.]

**A VISIT FROM SAINT NICHOLAS.**

CLEMENT C. MOORE.

A 1857 *Harper's New Monthly Magazine* cover with Santa and reindeer illustration for Clement C. Moore's *A Visit From Saint Nicolas* aka *'Twas the Night Before Christmas* poem. Illustrated by Felix Octavius Carr Darley.

1857 Illustrations in *Harpers Weekly* show Santa in various poses. On the top left, Santa looks on with a one-horse open sleigh, hot air balloon, and sail boat nearby. Bottom left is Santa sailing as swimmer's keep up pace with the boat. On the right is santa in his fur-lined coat, white beard, and Santa hat, ice skating while touching his nose. Source: *Harper's Weekly*, Vol. 7, (December 26, 1857), 821 (artist unknown).

In conclusion of Part I, I present to you three delightful illustrations of Santa by Thomas Nast on the following pages, two of which are his first published illustrated Santa's. Based on his 1881 Santa drawing, it is often said Nast created the Santa we know today, however, Jolly Santa with his white beard, warm smile, and fur-trimmed coat was established 1857 as illustrations on the previous pages demonstrate. I doubt anyone would disagree, though, Thomas Nast contributed memorable and lasting images of Santa. To view a complete collection of Thomas Nast Christmas artwork, look for my upcoming release: *A Very Thomas Nast Christmas*.

And now, I would like to present an eloquent quote about the tradition of Santa Claus by DeBow from 1868:

"Old Santa Claus! who does not feel a thrill of delight quivering through his heart as his eye meets the name of the patron Saint of his childhood? With the tones of long hushed Christmas bells, with the sweet laugh and expectant faces of little children, with the crackling fire and blazing logs in wide old country chimneys, with wonderful tales of reindeer steeds and toy laden sledges, with unfailing kindness and generosity and jollity lives old Santa Claus in the memory of those whose days of their youth are among the things that were."[23]

-Juleanne

---

[23] J. D. B. DeBow, *De Bow's Review,* "Art. XIV.—Christmas and Old Santa Claus," 1868, 1116-17.

Part I: Early History of Santa and His Reindeer

Thomas Nast's FIRST Santa Illustrations. Source: Top image: *Harper's Weekly,* Vol. 12, No. 314, January 3, 1863 (cover). Bottom: same edition, p. 13. Note: Though a Thomas Nast biographer (*Th. Nast, His Period and His Pictures,* 1904, p. 94) identified his first Santa as another published in *Christmas Poem's and Illustrations,* 1864, clearly the *Harper's Weekly* were first.

"Santa Claus, Merry Christmas," By Thomas Nast (signed 1884).
Source: *Harper's Bazar*, January 3, 1885, Vol. XVIII-No. 1.

Part I: Early History of Santa and His Reindeer

Thomas Nast's "Merry Old Santa Claus." In black and white and spread out on two pages of *Harper's Weekly*, it quickly became one of the most famous drawings of Santa.
Source: "Merry Old Santa Claus," *Harper's Weekly*, Vol XXV., No. 1253, January 1, 1881, 8-9.

# PART II

## Part II: Rare 1821 Children's Friend With Old Santeclaus

## Introduction to Part II: 1821 Children's Friend

In *Part II: 1821 Children's Friend* you will find an extremely rare, illustrated poem that likely influenced Clement Clarke Moore in writing *'Twas the Night*. It was the first known publication to illustrate Santa with his sleigh and a single, flying reindeer. Although accompanying drawings show a thin St. Nicholas holding a bishop's sceptor, or rod, his hat reads 'Santeclaus' and instead of referring to St. Nicholas Day on December 6th, the poem has Santa arriving for the first time on Christmas Eve.

*The Children's Friend, Number III: A New-Year's Present, to the Little Ones from Five to Twelve Part III* is the third in a special 'Children's Friend' series, published by William B. Gilley. It is believed to be the <u>first</u> American Christmas picture book. There are only <u>two known copies</u> in the world, one of which is located at American Antiquarian Society in Worcester, Massachusetts.[24]

This wonderful Christmas keepsake features a delightful poem called *Old Santeclaus With Much Delight*. The poem's author is anonymous and includes color illustrations by Rev. Arthur J. Stansbury (1781-1865), who in 1848 sketched President John Quincy Adams as he lay unconscious in the Rotunda of the Capitol at Washington after suffering a stroke.[25]

*Children's Friend* is reported to be the first time hand-colored lithographs were featured in a book in America. Isaac Doolittle and William Armand Barnet, the lithographers, established the first commercial lithographic printing shop in the United States.[26]

---

[24] Diann Benti, "Santa Claus Exposed," *Past is Present, the American Antiquarian Society blog*, December 14, 2009, *https://pastispresent.org/2009/good-sources/santa-claus-exposed/*.

[25] Arthur J. Stansbury, "The original sketch of Mr. Adams, taken when dying by A.J.S. in the Rotunda of the Capitol at Washington, 1848, *Library of Congress*, May 16, 2019, *https://www.loc.gov/pictures/item/97504745/*.

[26] David Tatham, ed, *Prints and Printmakers of New York State, 1825-1940*, (New York: Syracuse University Press, 1986) 8.

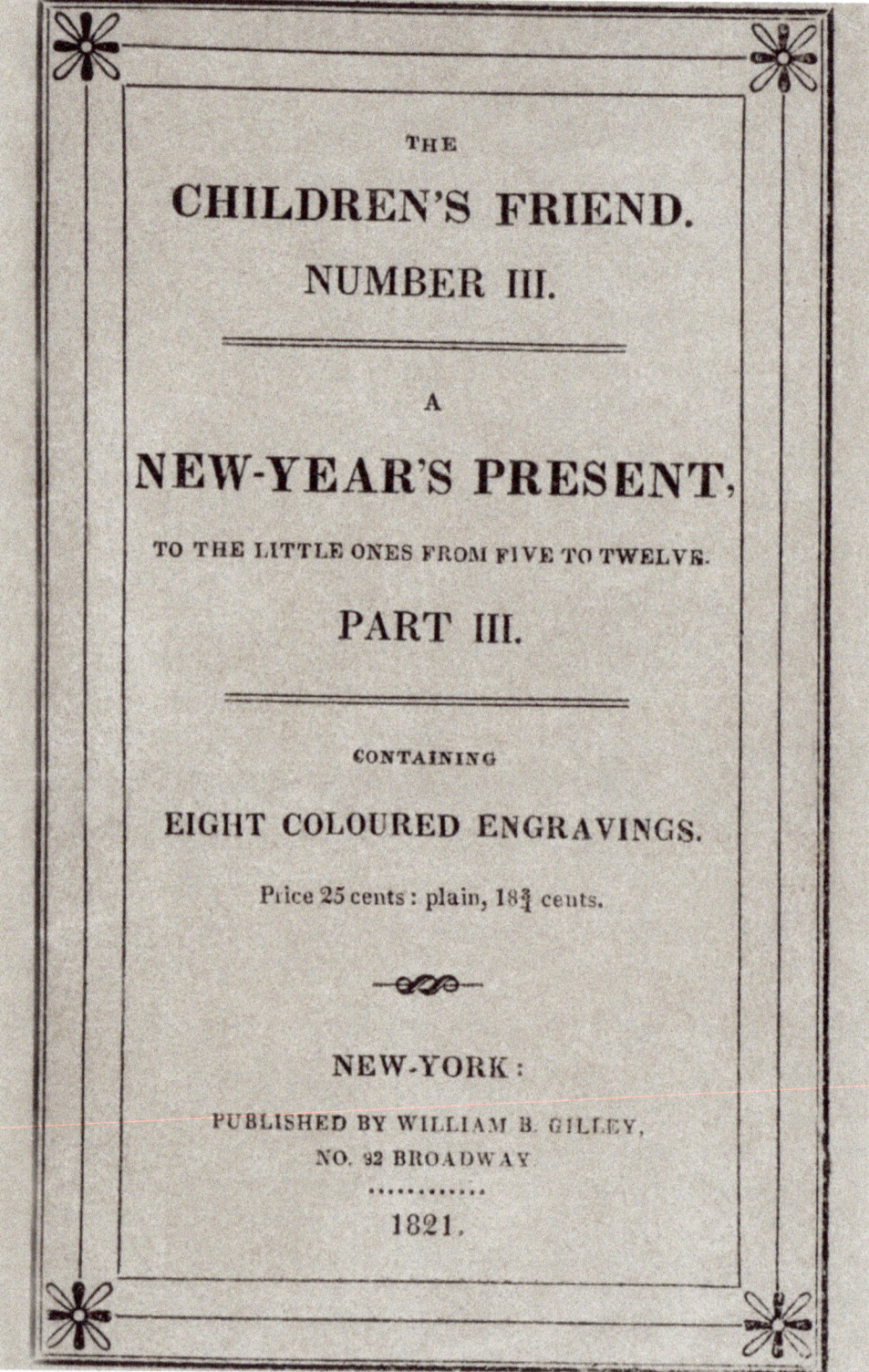

Old Santeclaus with much delight

His reindeer drives this frosty night,

O'er chimney tops, and tracks of snow,

To bring his yearly gifts to you.

The steady friend of virtuous youth,

The friend of duty, and of truth,

Each Christmas eve he joys to come

Where love and peace have made their home.

Through many houses he has been,
And various beds and stockings seen;
Some, white as snow, and neatly mended,
Others, that seem'd for pigs intended.

Where e'er I found good girls or boys,

That hated quarrels, strife and noise,

I left an apple, or a tart,

Or wooden gun, or painted cart;

To some I gave a pretty doll,

To some a peg-top, or a ball;

No crackers, cannons, squibs, or rockets,

To blow their eyes up, or their pockets.

No drums to stun their Mother's ear,

Nor swords to make their sisters fear;

But pretty books to store their mind

With knowledge of each various kind.

But where I found the children naughty,

In manners rude, in temper haughty,

Thankless to parents, liars, swearers,

Boxers, or cheats, or base tale-bearers,

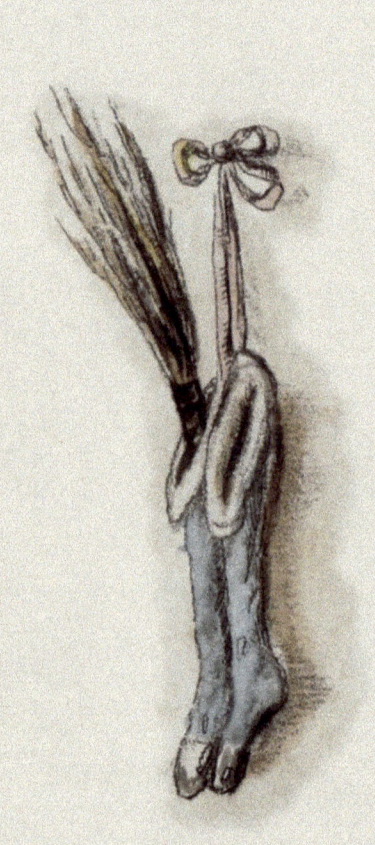

I left a long, black, birchen rod,

Such as the dread command of God

Directs a Parent's hand to use

When virtue's path his sons refuse.

## Part II: Rare 1821 Children's Friend With Old Santeclaus

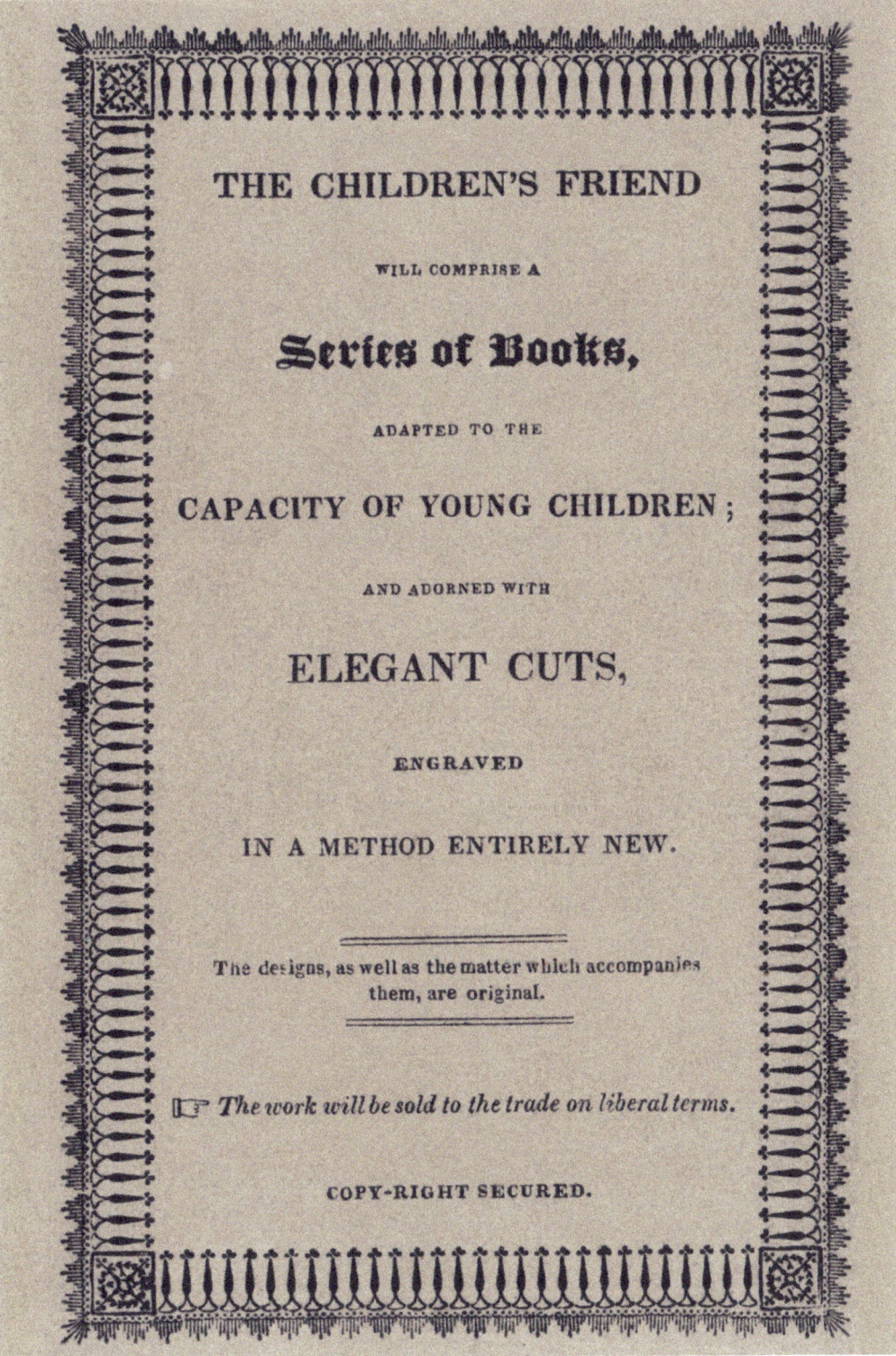

# 'TWAS THE NIGHT SERIES

## BOOK 1

***'Twas the Night Before Christmas: Early Santa History Plus Rare 1821 Children's Friend With Old Santeclaus*** provides an early history of Santa Claus and his reindeer, and includes the extremely rare, illustrated book written in 1821 called *Children's Friend: A New-Year's Present, to the Little Ones From Five to Twelve, Part III*. These were the inspiration behind the all-time favorite Christmas poem 'Twas the Night Before Christmas. *Children's Friend* has the first known Santa images in his sleigh pulled by a a single flying reindeer. There are only two known copies of this rare book which includes a poem called *Old Santeclaus With Much Delight*.

## BOOK 2

***'Twas the Night Before Christmas: Original 1823 Visit From St. Nicholas, History of Its Author, and Early Santa Illustrations*** includes the 1823 version of *A Visit from St. Nicholas* aka *'Twas the Night Before Christmas* poem and its history, controversy of the author, and a short biography of Moore.

## BOOK 3

***'Twas the Night Before Christmas: 1848 Visit From St. Nicholas, Illustrated*** features Moore's 1848 *A Visit From St. Nicholas* with color illustrations by Theodore Chauncy Boyd, and a short biography of Boyd.

BOOK 4

*'Twas the Night Before Christmas: 1862 Visit From St. Nicholas With Clement Moore's Handwritten Poem, Illustrated* includes Moore's 1862, color illustrated poem, and a copy of his handwritten poem made just one year before his death, signed and dated March 13, 1862.

Coming soon: *A Merry Thomas Nast Christmas*, featuring his Christmas drawings and a short biography of the talented artist.

All my best,
Juleanne

# Bibliography

Baring-Gould, S. *The Lives of the Saints*. London: John Hodges, 1877.

Benti, Diann. "Santa Claus Exposed." *Past is Present, the American Antiquarian Society blog*. December 14, 2009. https://pastispresent.org/2009/good-sources/santa-claus-exposed/.

Brewer, Ebenezer Cobham. A Dictionary of Miracles: Imitative, Realistic, and Dogmatic with Illustrations. Philadelphia, PA: J. B. Lippincott Company, 1894.

Butler, Alban Rev., *The Lives of the Fathers Martyrs, and Other Principal Saints; Compiled from Original Monuments, and other Authentic Records, Illustrated with The Remarks of Judiciuos Modern Critics and Historians, Vol. II*, London: Joseph Booker, 1833.

Chapin, Emily. "Clement Clarke Moore and Santa in the City," *Museum of the City of New York*. November 29, 2016. 222.mcny.org/story/clement-clarke-moore-and-santa-city.

Cooper, Susan Fenimore. *Rural Hours by a Lady*. New York: George P. Putnam, 1850.

DeBow, J.D.B. *De Bow's Review*, "Art. XIV.—Christmas and Old Santa Claus," 1868.

Hoffman, Charles Fenno. *New-York Book of Poetry*. New York: George Dearborn, 1837.

"Holiday Greeting, Our Annual Supplement (supplement to the Thibodaux L.A. Sentinel)." *The Weekly Thibodaux Sentinel and Journal of the 8th Senatorial District*, December 26, 1891.

Irving, Washington (writing as Diedrich Knickerbocker). *A History of New-York From the Beginning of the World to the End of the Dutch Dynasty, Volumes I and II*. New York: Inskeep & Bradford, 1809.

Irving, Washington [writing as Diedrich Knickerbocker]. *Salmagundi: or, The Whim=Whams and Opinions of Launcelot Langstaff, Esq. and Others* [No. XX-Monday, January 25, 1808 "From My Elbow Chair"]. London: T. Davison, Whitefriars, 1824.

Jones, Charles W. "Knickerbocker Santa Claus." *St. Nicholas Center.* May 16, 2019. www.stnicholascenter.org/who-is-st-nicholas/origin-of-santa/kickerbocker.

Kaller, Seth. "Appendix C: Historical Timeline." *Seth Kaller, Inc.* May 12, 2019. www.sethkaller.com/about/educational/tnbc-2.

Keese, John. *The Poets of America: Illustrated by One of Her Painters.* New York: S. Colman, 1840.

Moore, Clement C., LL. D. *Poems.* New York: Bartlett & Welford, 1844.

Moore, Clement Clarke, author, and Nast, Thomas, Illustrator. *Visit of St. Nicholas, Aunt Louisa's Big Picture Series.* New York, McLoughlin Bros, circa 1872.

Nissenbaum, Stephen. *The Battle for Christmas: A Social and Cultural History of our Most Cherished Holiday.* New York: Vintage, a Division of Random House, Inc., 1996.

Norsworthy, Scott. "First printing of A Visit from St. Nicholas," *Melvilliana*. April 8, 2019. https://melvilliana.blogspot.com/2019/04/first-printing-of-visit-from-st-nicholas.html.

Paulding, James K. *The Story Book of Saint Nicholas Translated From the Original Dutch of Dominie Nicholas Aegidius Oudenarde.* New York: Harper & Brothers, 1836.

Restad, Penne L. *Christmas in America: A History.* New York: Oxford University Press, 1995.

"Santa Claus." *History*. July 6, 2019. www.history.com/topics/christmas/santa-claus.

Stansbury, Arthur J., illustrator. *The Children's Friend. Number III.: A New-Year's present, to the little ones from five to twelve. Part III.* New York, William B. Gilley, 1821.

Stansbury, Arthur J. "The original sketch of Mr. Adams, taken when dying by A.J.S. in the Rotunda of the Capitol at Washington, 1848. May 16, 2019. *Library of Congress, https://www.loc.gov/pictures/item/97504745/*.

Tatham, David, ed. *Prints and Printmakers of New York State, 1825-1940.* New York: Syracuse University Press, 1986.

Willmott, Robert Aris, ed. *The Poets of the Nineteenth Century.* London: George Routledge & Co, 1857.

www.ingramcontent.com/pod-product-compliance
Lightning Source LLC
Chambersburg PA
CBHW051350110526
44591CB00025B/2956